BEER LOVER'S COLORING BOOK

Join our mailing list to be among

the first to find out about special offers,

discounts and our new releases!

Sign up at:
www.adultcoloringworld.net

@adultcoloringworld

facebook.com/adultcoloringworldbooks

@adultcolorworld

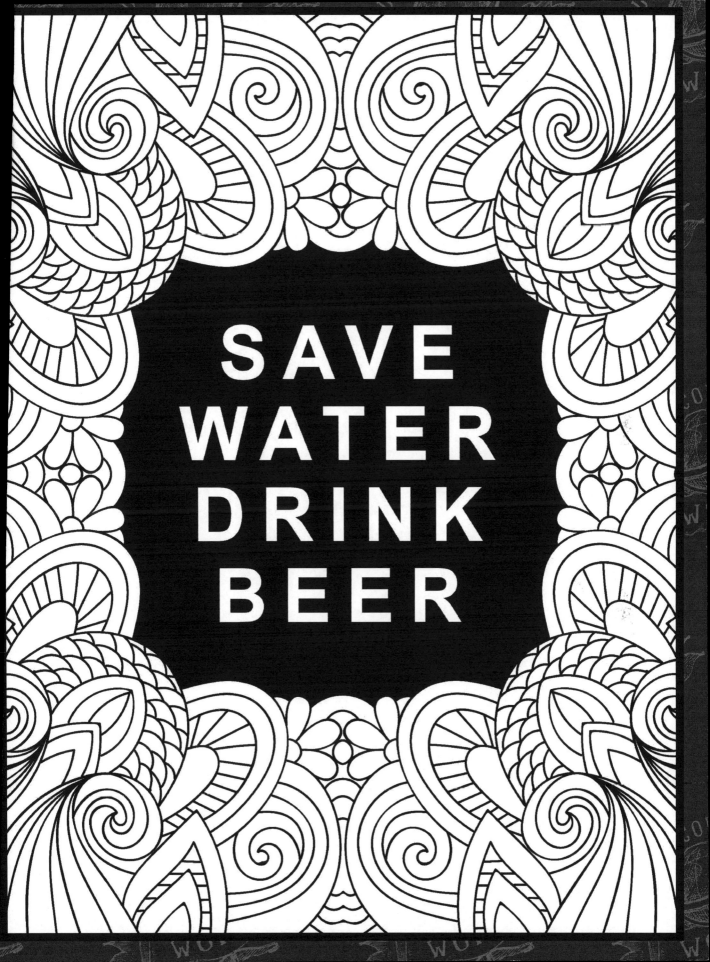

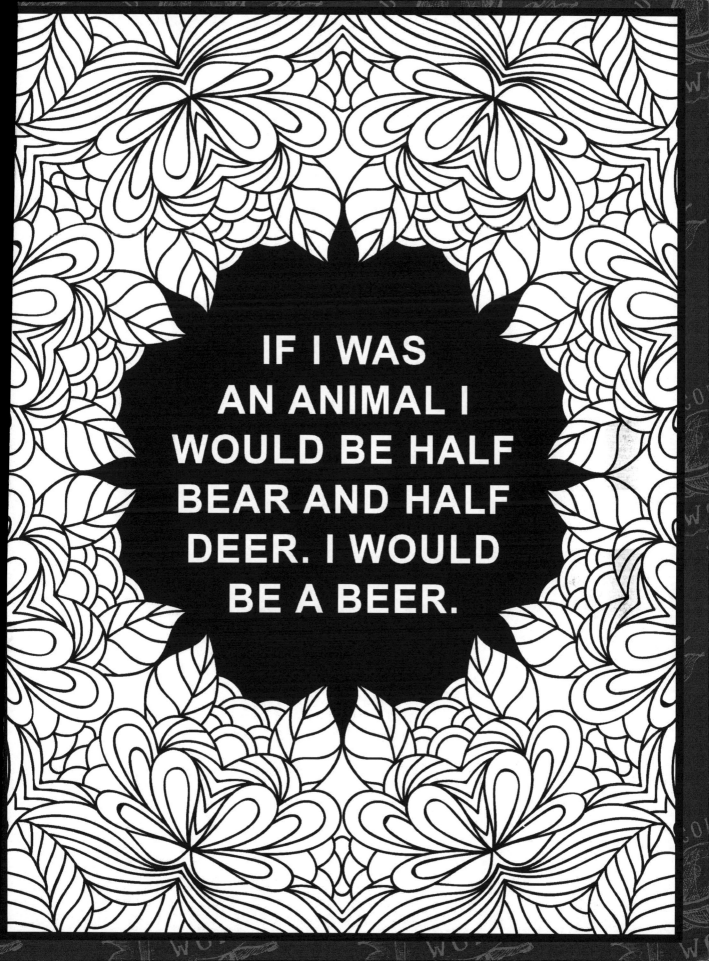

IF I WAS
AN ANIMAL I
WOULD BE HALF
BEAR AND HALF
DEER. I WOULD
BE A BEER.

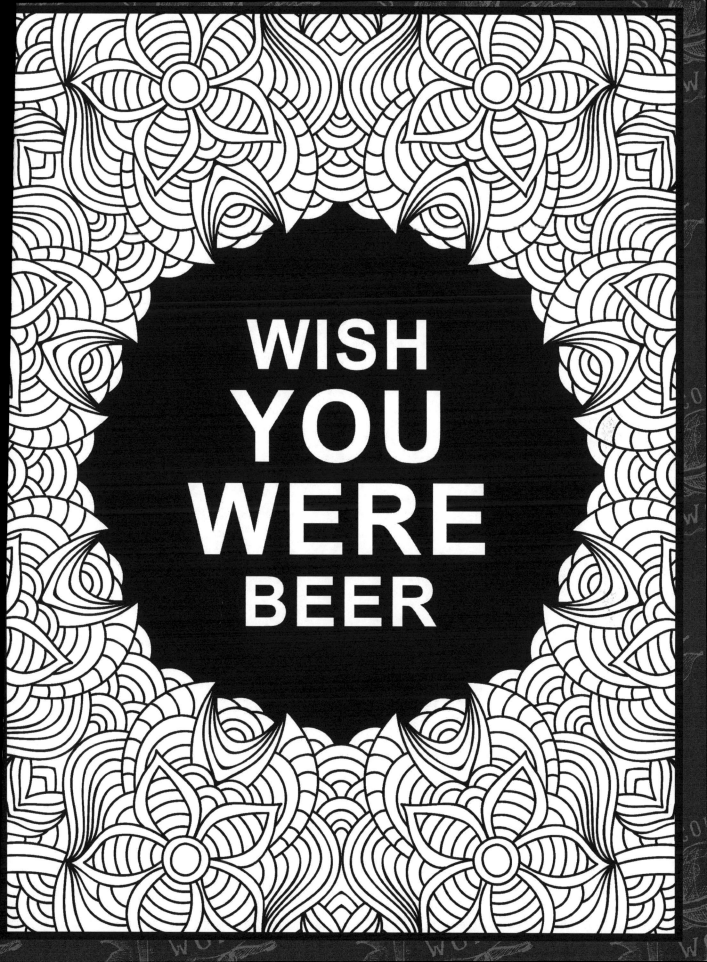

I GOT
THIS BODY
GOING ON
BEER RUNS

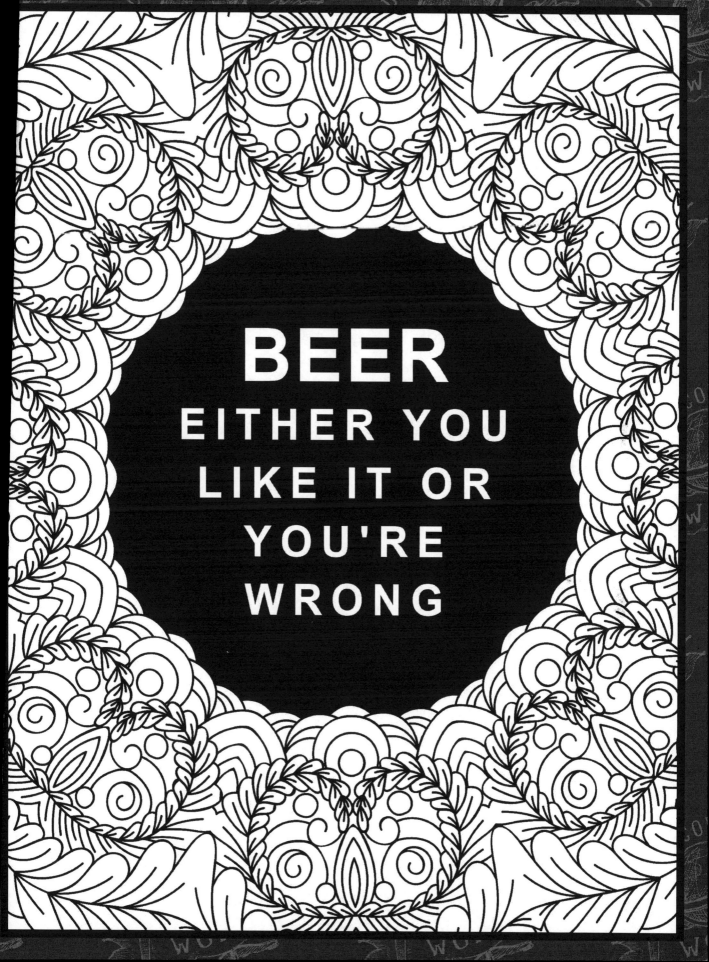

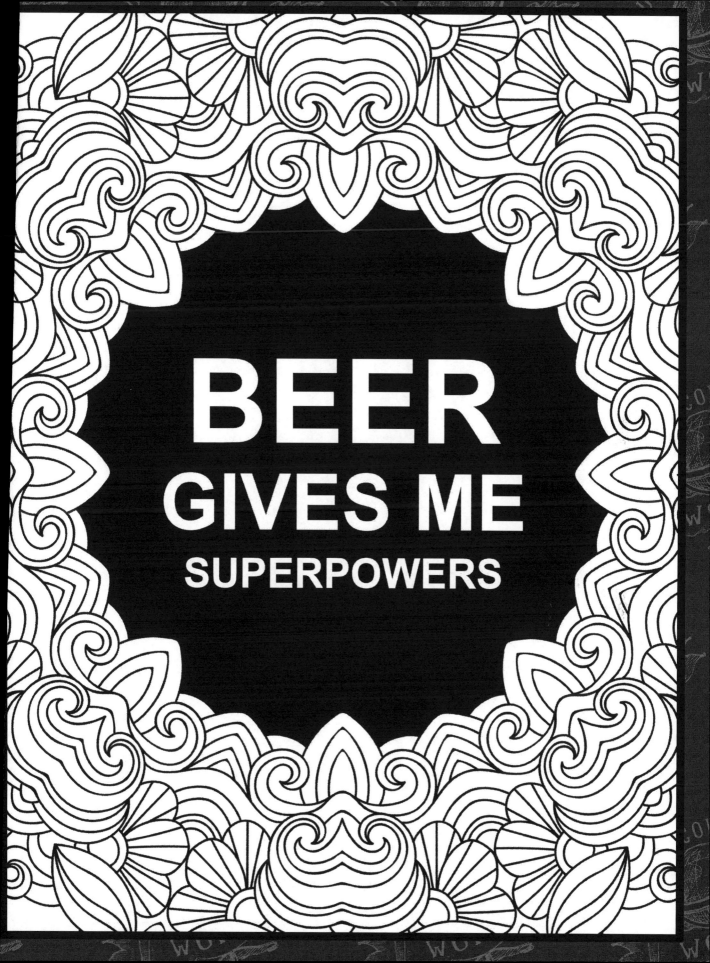

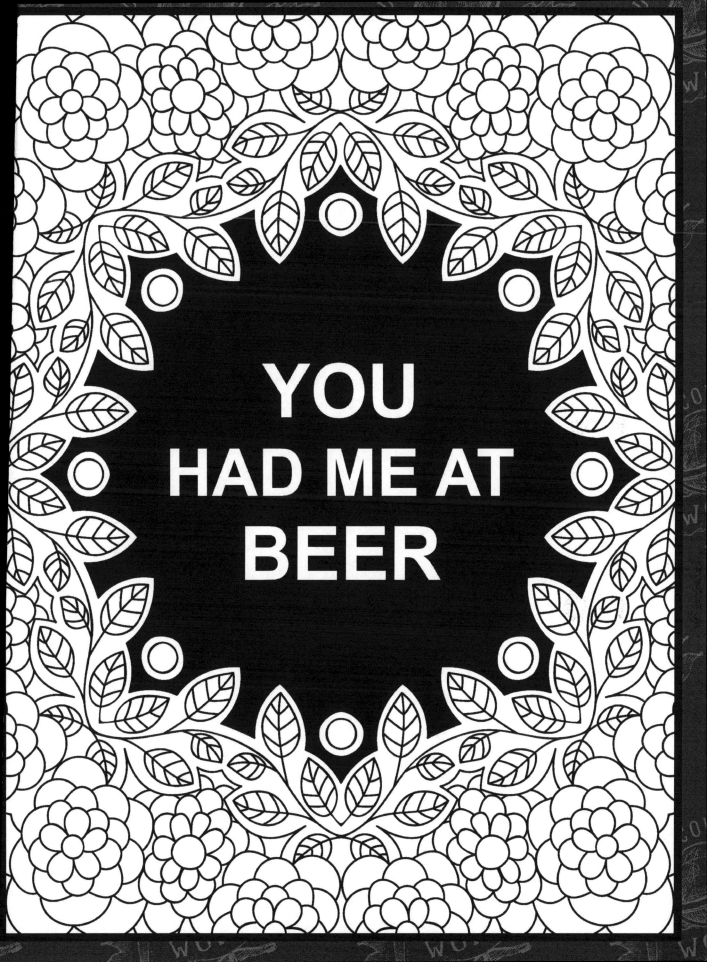

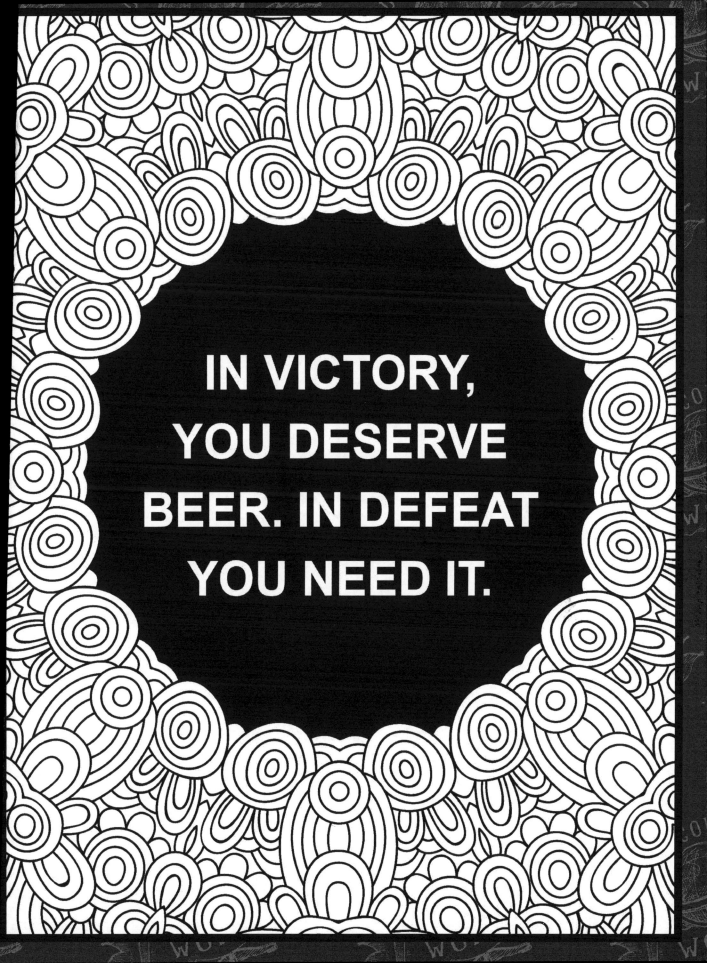

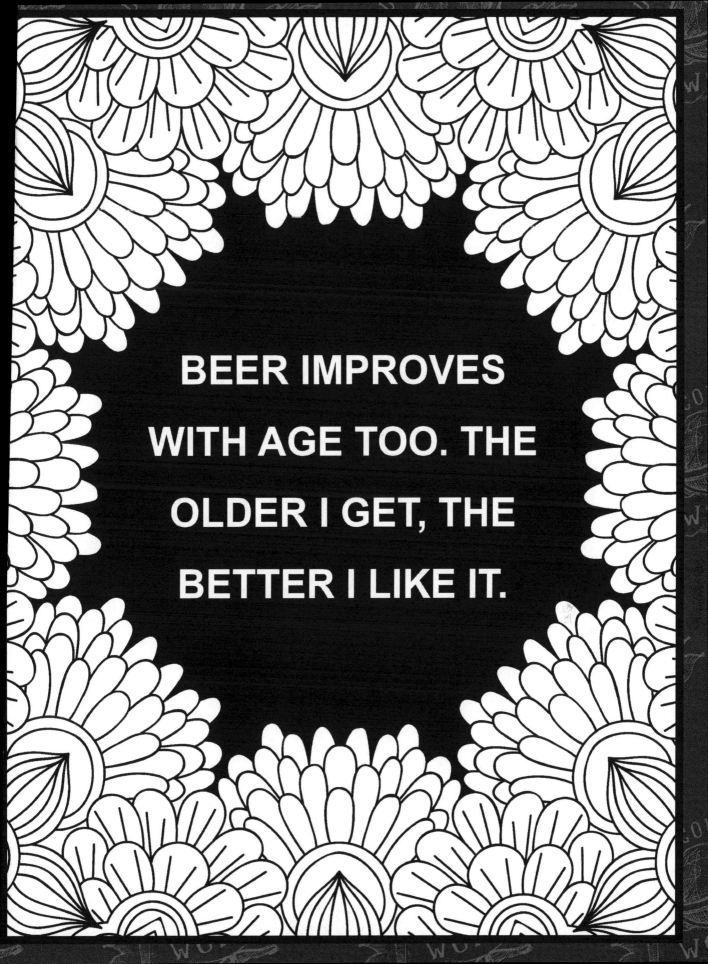

BEER IMPROVES WITH AGE TOO. THE OLDER I GET, THE BETTER I LIKE IT.

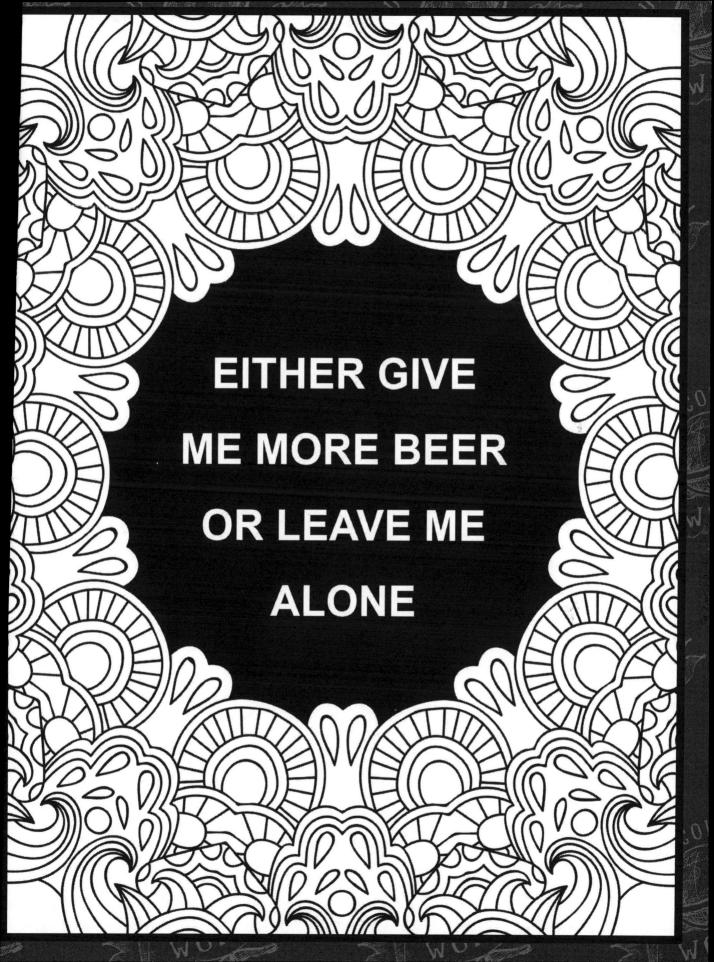

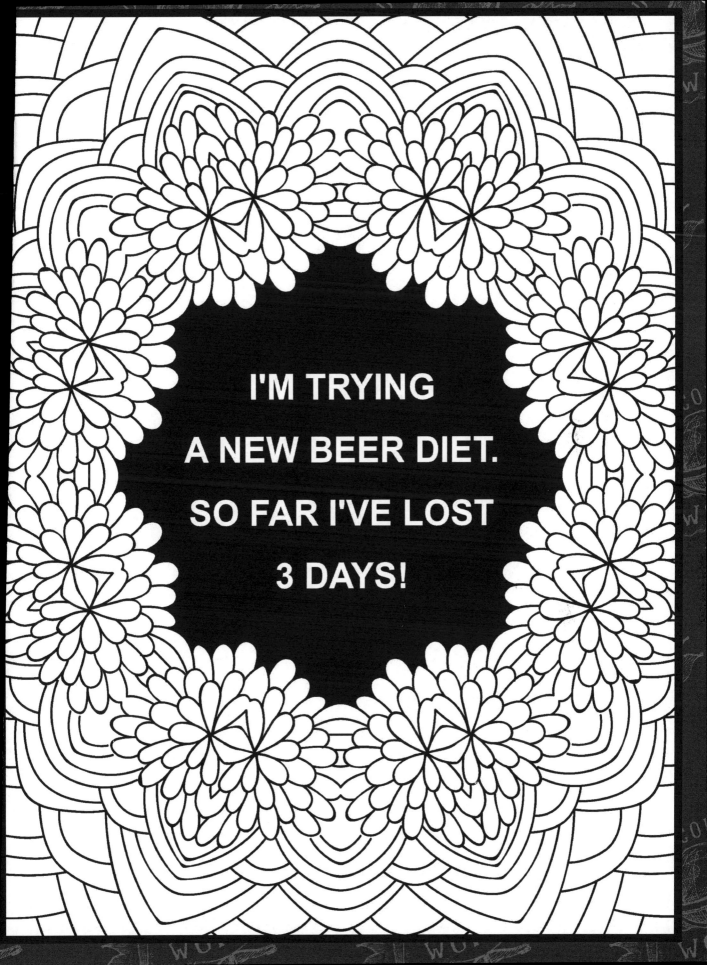

DRINK BEER:

IT ISN'T GOOD TO

KEEP THINGS

BOTTLED UP

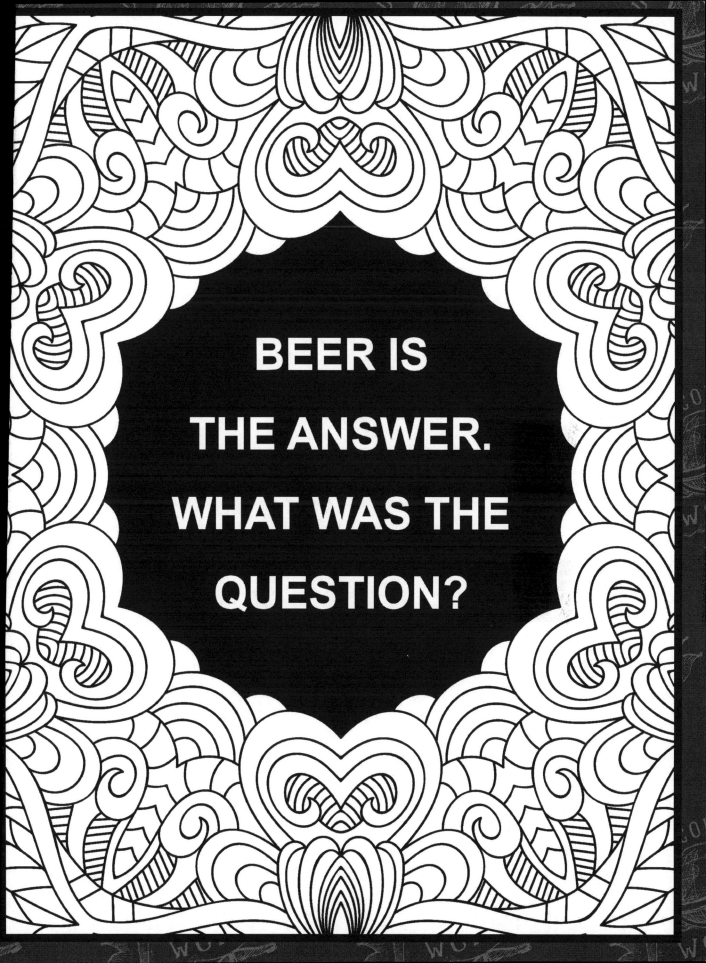

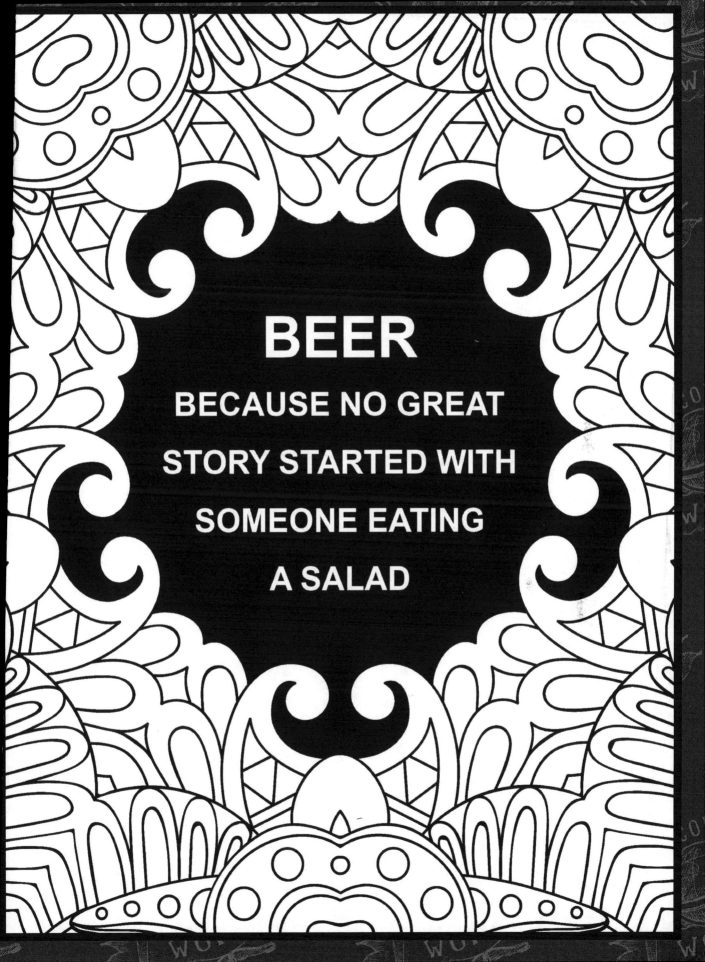

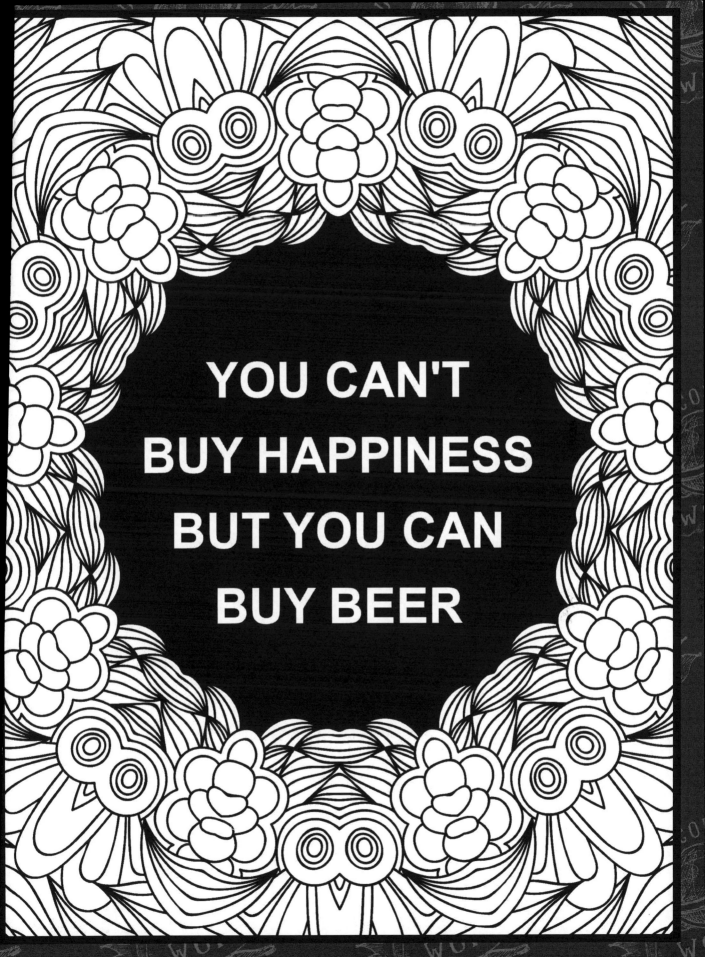

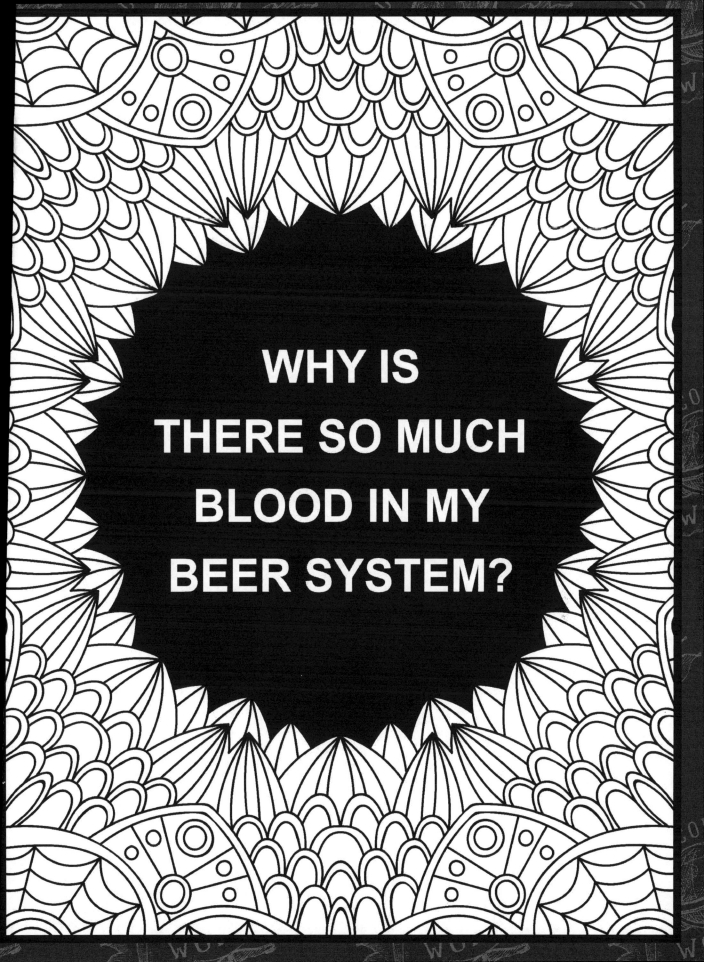

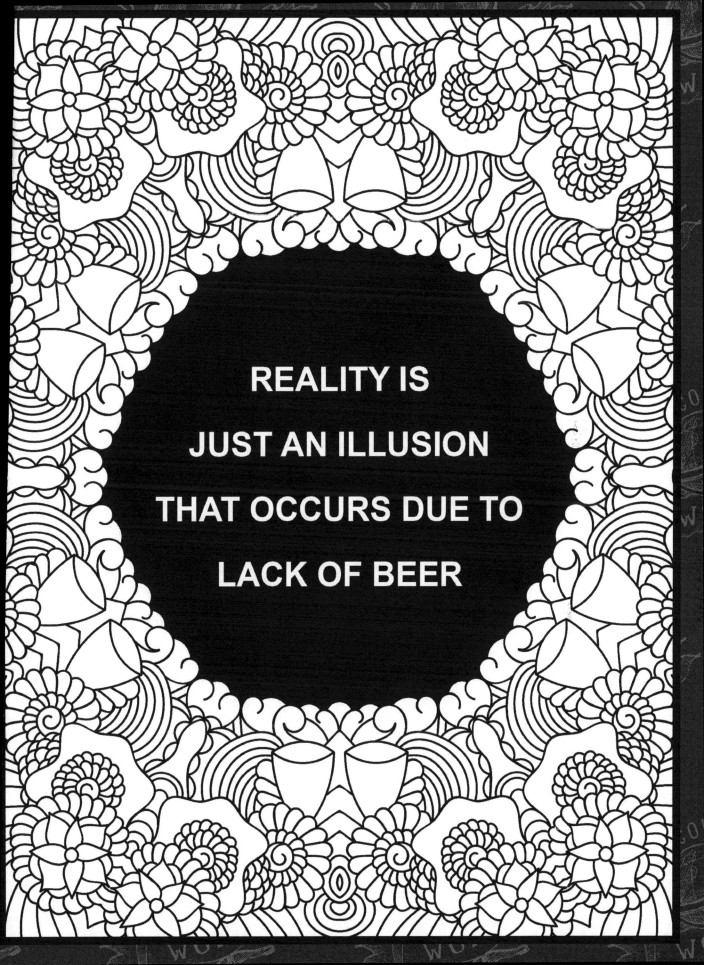

REALITY IS
JUST AN ILLUSION
THAT OCCURS DUE TO
LACK OF BEER

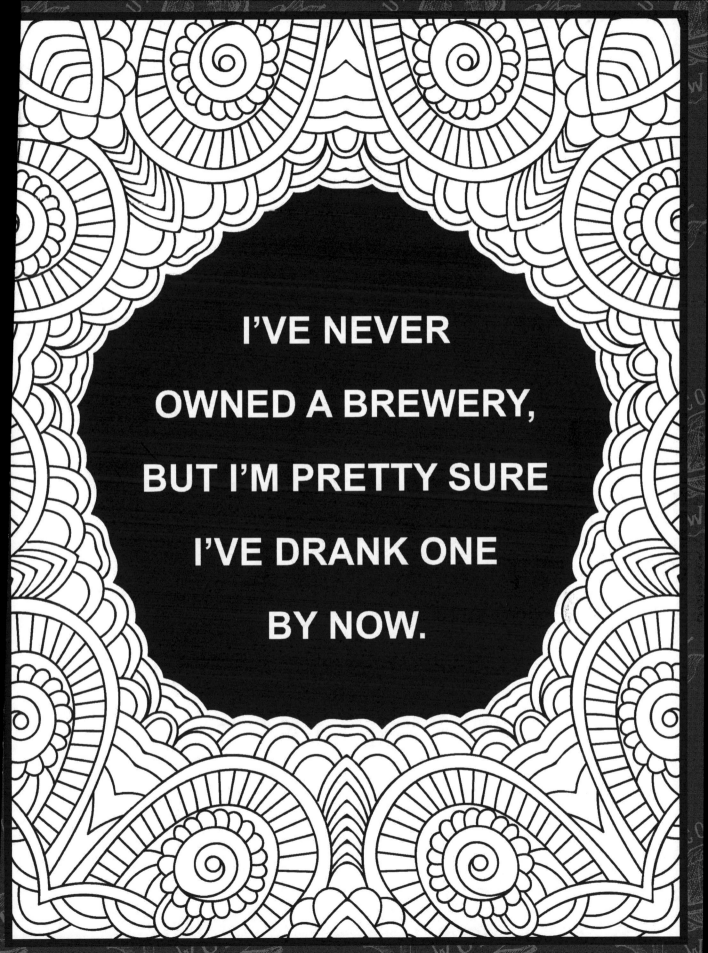

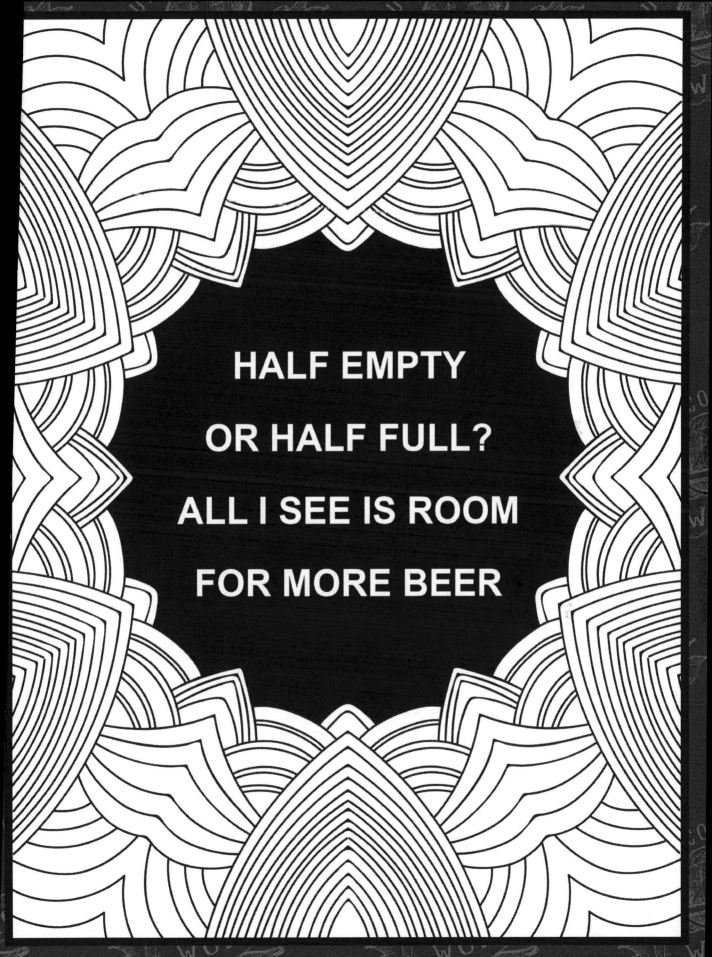

I THINK
MY CHECK LIVER
LIGHT IS ABOUT
TO COME ON

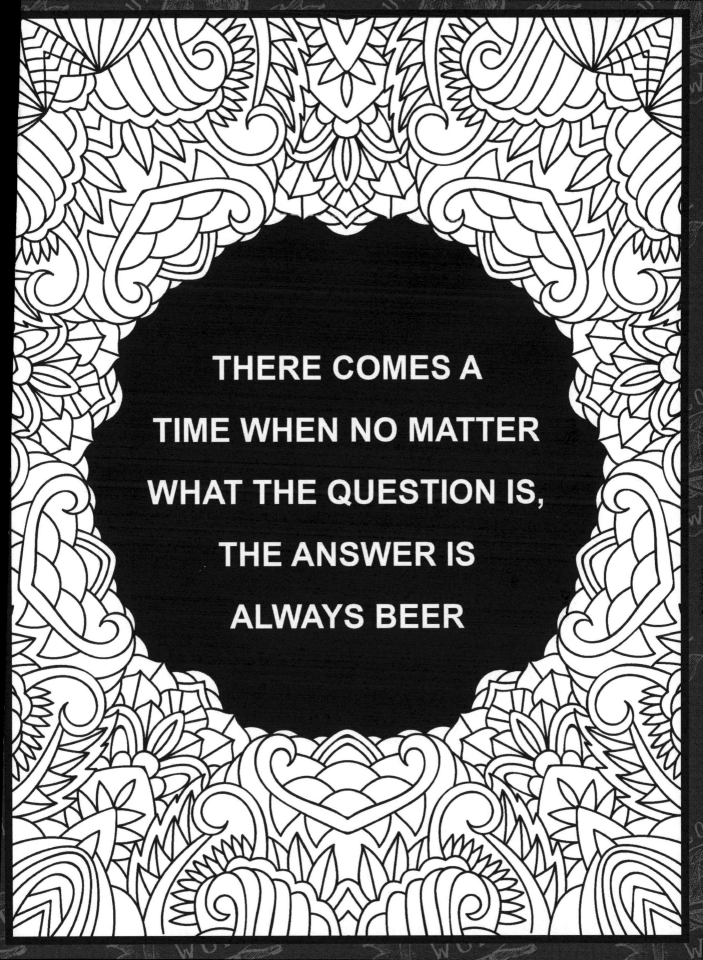

THERE COMES A
TIME WHEN NO MATTER
WHAT THE QUESTION IS,
THE ANSWER IS
ALWAYS BEER

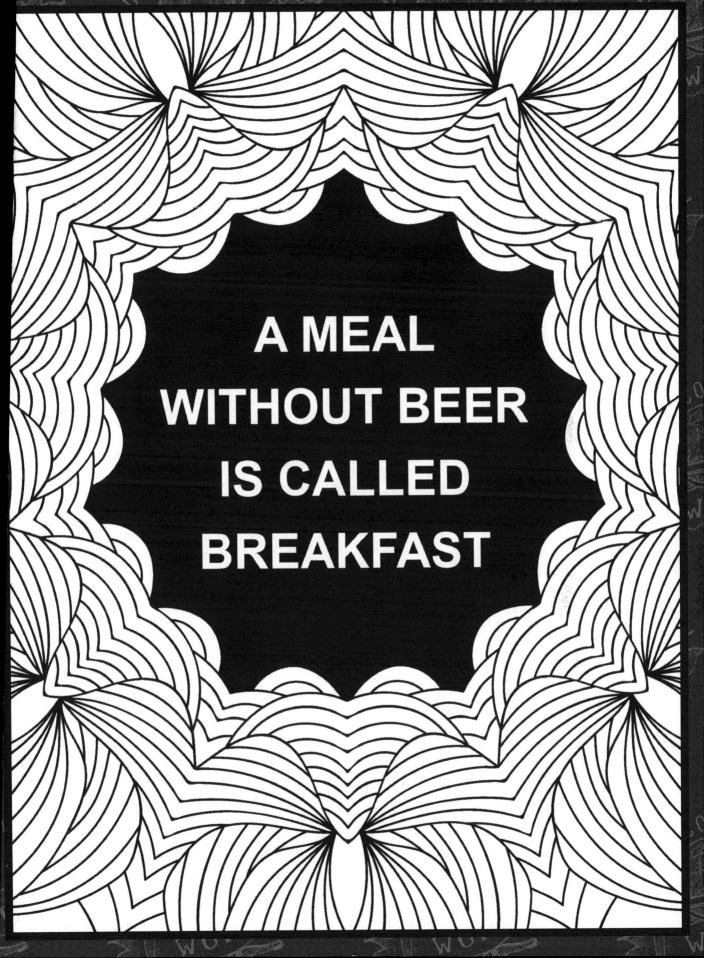

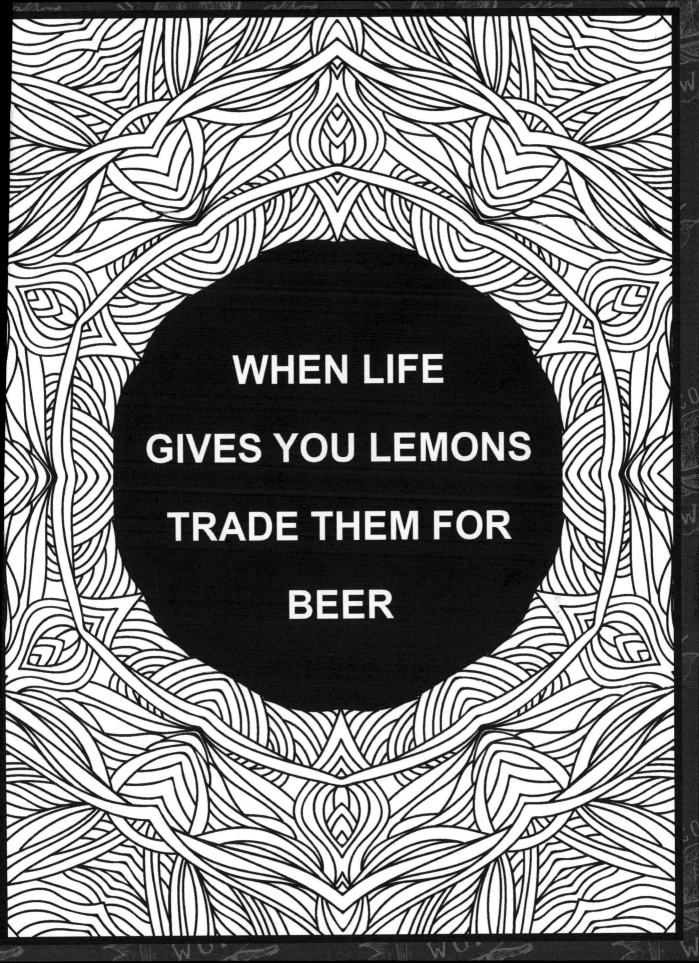

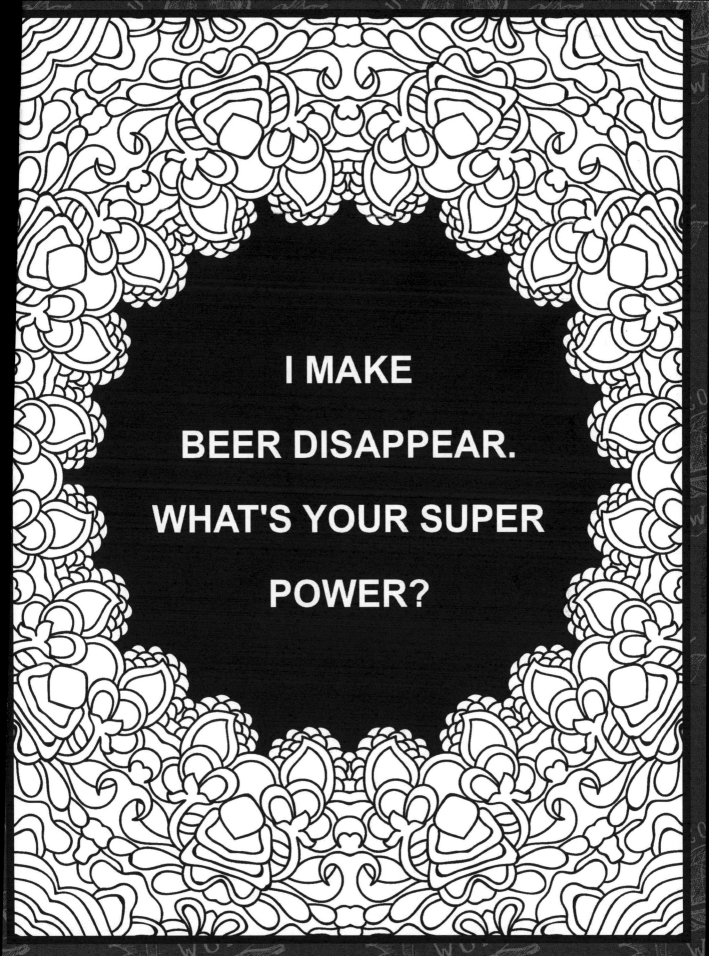

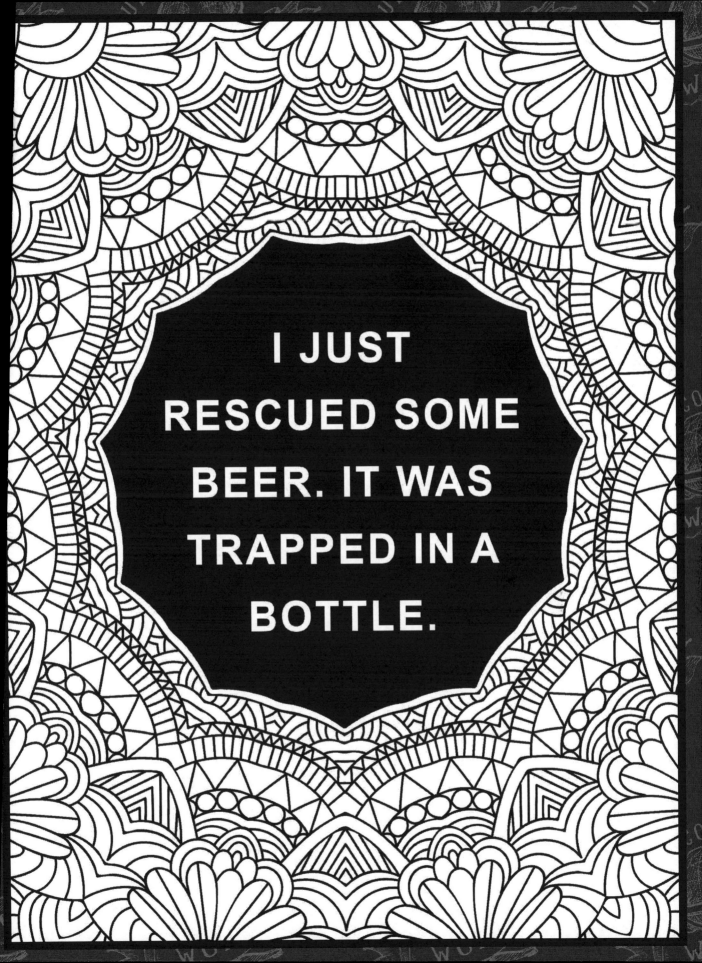

COLOR TEST
PAGE

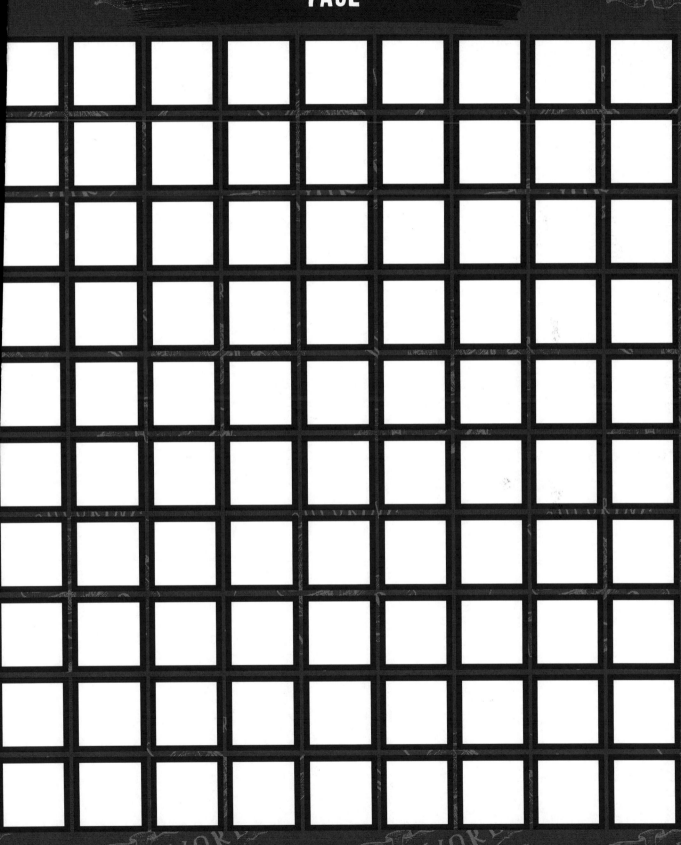

COLOR TEST PAGE

COLOR TEST PAGE

WE HOPE YOU
ENJOYED THIS BOOK!

TO VIEW OUR HUGE
RANGE OF ADULT COLORING
BOOKS, VISIT OUR WEBSITE
TODAY AND DON'T FORGET
TO FOLLOW US VIA OUR
SOCIAL ACCOUNTS!

ADULTCOLORINGWORLD.NET

Made in the USA
Middletown, DE
21 November 2018